D0455885

50 WAYS
TO HELP THE
PLANET

SIÂN BERRY

Kyle Books

Dolores County Public Library
PO Box 578
Dove Creek, CO 81324-0578

ABOUT THE AUTHOR

Siân Berry is co-leader of the Green Party. She has been a campaigner and politician on green issues since 2001, starting out as a local Green Party candidate in 2002 and co-founding a successful campaign to change attitudes to urban 4x4 vehicles. After turning to green activism full-time, she worked as a transport campaigner for a charity until 2016 when she was elected to the London Assembly. Siân stood for Mayor of London for the Greens in 2008 and again in 2016, coming third.

Siân is also elected as a councillor in the London borough of Camden, and she campaigns across London on the housing crisis, youth services, civil liberties, air pollution and green spaces. In her local area, she has challenged policies on green energy, regeneration, local shops and traffic.

She studied engineering at university and worked professionally in marketing and communications before turning to green issues. These skills give her a straightforward and accessible approach to promoting more sustainable policies and choices, focusing on what people can do today to make a difference, and what governments need to do to make greener lives easier and cheaper for everyone.

As a well-known figure in green campaigning and politics, Siân has received wide coverage in national and international newspapers and is a regular contributor to a range of TV and radio programmes.

CONTENTS

An Hachette UK Company
www.hachette.co.uk

First published in Great Britain in 2018 by
Kyle Books, an imprint of Kyle Cathie Ltd
Carmelite House, 50 Victoria Embankment
London, EC4Y 0DZ
www.kylebooks.co.uk

ISBN: 978 0 85783 5147

Text copyright 2018 © Siân Berry
Design and layout copyright 2018 © Aaron Blecha
Artwork copyright 2018 © Aaron Blecha

Distributed in the US by Hachette Book Group,
1290 Avenue of the Americas, 4th and 5th Floors, New York, NY 10104

Distributed in Canada by Canadian Manda Group,
664 Annette St., Toronto, Ontario, Canada M6S 2C8

Siân Berry is hereby identified as the author of this work in accordance with
Section 77 of the Copyright, Designs and Patents Act 1988.

All rights reserved. No part of this work may be reproduced or utilised in any
form or by any means, electronic or mechanical, including photocopying, recording
or by any information storage and retrieval system, without the prior written
permission of the publisher.

Editors: Muna Reyal, Isabel Gonzalez-Prendergast & Judith Hannam
Designer and Illustrator: Aaron Blecha

A Cataloguing in Publication record for this title is available from the British Library

Printed and bound in China

10 9 8 7 6 5 4 3 2

MIX
Paper from
responsible sources
FSC® C144853
www.fsc.org

FEAR THRIVES IN THE EMPTY
SPACES THAT EMERGE WHEN
PEOPLE ARE SEPARATE. HOPE
THRIVES WHEN WE CONNECT
WITH OUR NEIGHBOURS AND
WITH OUR NATURAL WORLD.
THIS IS HOW WE ALL SURVIVE
– WE MAKE CONNECTIONS,
WE SEED HOPE. WE LOOK
FORWARD NOT BACKWARDS.
AND TOGETHER WE WRITE A
BETTER FUTURE.

Caroline Lucas

PLASTICS

Plastic recycling is usually the first thing that comes to mind when we think about being green, and the enormous amount of damage to the world's oceans caused by carelessly discarded plastics has now put these issues right at the top of our concerns again.

This is thanks to effective campaigns from groups like Greenpeace, as well as television programmes showing our seas filled with pieces of plastic causing wildlife the most awful and heartbreaking injuries. At the same time, microscopic plastic particles broken down from the bottles and packaging we discard are affecting even the smallest sea creatures. The delicate balance of our planet just can't cope with the amount of plastic waste we're putting out into the environment, and we need to act urgently to prevent further harm.

As a society, we need manufacturers and governments to step up and stop the production of some of the most harmful plastic products, such as 'microbeads' in cosmetics, but as individuals we can also play our part.

Most of us are aware of the need to recycle, but we are improving our efforts far too slowly. In the UK, we're way behind some other countries that have had policies like bottle deposit schemes for years. Our recycling rates in most places are barely rising and, in some areas, we are even going backwards.

We know that recycling is not the only answer. There's a growing movement to reduce and re-use the plastic used in daily life, which can only be positive as we work towards a zero-waste culture and try not to make the damage we've done so far even worse.

TAKE HOME LESS PLASTIC

Around one fifth of household waste is food packaging. A good way to start cutting back on plastic waste, therefore, is to reduce the amount of unnecessary material we bring home.

Some European countries let you leave excess packaging in the shop for the company to recycle. If you're feeling militant, you could try to implement this at your local supermarket! If not, then try these simple ideas.

• Always make sure you carry enough reusable shopping bags for your trips to the shops.
• Choose food that comes unwrapped, particularly fresh fruit and vegetables. Use the fish, butcher and deli counters to get fresh foods wrapped in paper rather than plastic pre-packs.
• Use local bakeries for really fresh bread and pastries that come home in paper bags and boxes. Shopping locally helps the planet in other ways, too – see tip 47 (Back Your Local High Street).
• Look out for products that have switched to non-plastic alternatives, such as corn starch, bamboo and cardboard as a substitute for plastic wrappers, boxes and trays.
• I was shocked to find that most brands of tea bags also contain plastic woven into the fibres, making it impossible to recycle and really hazardous in the ecosystem. Until more brands change their ways, try loose tea or the few that have already put alternatives in place.

2 DON'T GO DISPOSABLE

'Disposable' is a terrible word. As well as encouraging the wasteful use of resources, it also implies things can be thrown away without consequence. As a green, the growing number of one-use items in the world makes my blood boil.

I recommend you shun all the plastic-based disposable products you can. Whether it's a cleaning cloth or duster you 'simply throw away', a razor you use only a few times, or a coffee machine that uses a fancy pod every time you want a cup of coffee.

It's when eating on the go or at work that most of us encounter disposable items – those plastic trays, packets and cutlery in most takeaway restaurants, sandwich shops and coffee houses. One simple way to help is to take in a spoon, fork and knife to keep at your desk for everyday use. And use your consumer elbow to ask the places you buy from most often to switch to wood, starch or bamboo alternatives for their customers.

And don't forget your toothbrush – in the USA alone, around a billion plastic toothbrushes are thrown away every year and less than a fifth are recycled. Try the growing number of non-plastic alternatives, such as bamboo.

REFILL AND RE-USE 3

There was once a real culture of reusable bottles and packaging, with good systems in place to use them efficiently. When I was a little girl, milk, juice, fizzy drinks, bread and eggs were all sold door-to-door by providers who collected up empties when delivering new goods, but nowadays there are very few of these businesses around.

Concerns about waste mean that more new companies are springing up to fill this gap. Many cleaning products and cosmetics are now produced in refillable containers, and greener shops are emerging that sell refills for these products, along with dried goods like rice, cereals and coffee that you can take away in paper bags or your own containers. There are two of these shops within walking distance of my flat in London, so look out for any that start up near you, and help them grow by using them regularly.

You can also help by re-using packaging for a different purpose, such as storing homemade salad dressings and sauces, or for growing plants in the garden.

4 PLASTIC-FREE BEAUTY

Potions and products to help our hair and skin look, smell and feel better are a billion-dollar business, but they tend to be very heavy on the packaging. Most beauty products come in a liquid form, so transporting them uses up lots of fossil fuels, and excessive fancy packaging is half the selling point of many face creams, serums and perfumes.

Recent horror stories about 'fatbergs' in our sewers caused by plastic reinforced wipes being flushed down toilets, and the news that plastic 'microbeads' from cleansing products are polluting the oceans, have started to make us think again about our beauty regimes.

It's great that more companies now are producing products with a lower impact on the planet. Shops like Lush sell unpackaged soaps and other products, and will refill their bottles and tubs, giving incentives to close the loop. Brands are also helping to cut down on transport costs with innovative products like solid shampoos.

Smaller companies making similar efforts may not be as obvious on the high street, so make an effort to seek them out in places like health food stores. Most green brands will use natural ingredients and are cruelty-free for a really ethical clean-up.

GREENER WASHING 5

The average family uses their washing machine hundreds of times a year. This makes how we choose to wash our clothes a big source of plastics in our lives and a major choice in terms of the impact we have on the planet.

Choose concentrated detergents with less packaging per wash and buy the largest size you can each time. Also look for the greenest, lowest impact brands of detergent that don't contain enzymes or phosphates that can pollute our waters.

Replace fabric softener with a cup of clear vinegar added during the rinse cycle. This neutralises the soap and freshens clothes without using extra plastic-packaged products.

Saving energy and water when you wash is important too – see tips 17 (Green Machines) and 21 (Save Water in the Home) for how to get the most from your washing machine. Don't forget to reduce your washing temperature too: 30 degrees is plenty.

Hang things up to dry – outdoors whenever you can – rather than tumble drying. And avoid those extra freshness sheets in the dryer: like tea bags and single-use wash cloths, they may contain hidden plastics.

6 GREENER FIBRES

I was shocked to learn that many of the smallest shreds of plastic found in sea water samples come from our clothing. These 'microfibres' come from washing our clothes. They are shed through the friction of the wash and then go into the sewage system and out to sea, where they can have a huge impact on marine life. While clothes made of plastic-based fibres may be durable, these microfibres will pollute our seas for generations.

Future washing machines will need to have better filters now that we know about this problem. But meanwhile, you can get fine mesh bags to put your clothes in during the wash, which will capture the shreds and help keep them out of the oceans.

This is another good reason to look for natural, ethically-produced clothing in the shops. Greener product labels to look out for include organic and fair trade, and seek out the following fibres where you can.

Hemp – this crop needs very few nutrients and can be grown organically in most areas of the world. The fibres can be made into a wide range of fabric weights and the plant also produces oil and seeds for food.

Bamboo – this is a type of grass and is incredibly fast-growing, needing no artificial fertilisers in most areas. Bamboo can be used for many household articles and can also be made into hard-wearing fabrics.

Wool – if produced organically, this comes from sheep that are not dipped in chemicals and raised on land that is not overgrazed, ensuring that organic wool has a very low environmental impact.

Cotton – unfortunately cotton is a very resource-intensive crop, responsible for 12 per cent of global pesticide use. Many poor cotton farmers suffer the effects of agricultural chemicals yet don't make a fair living. Bringing fair trade and organic approaches to the cotton industry has the potential to improve the lives of huge numbers of people and protect the environment. Because of the high impact of cotton production, I always buy organic cotton where I can.

7 SLOW FASHION

'Fast fashion' is a recent term that criticises many of the larger shops for encouraging us to buy cheap clothes we'll only wear a few times.

I know all too well that feeling when you want something new and shiny to wear to a big event and you can't afford to pay a lot, but there are alternatives that are far better for the planet.

More than half of my clothes are second-hand, and hunting for good vintage items is one of my favourite things. These days fashion is much less rigid, and buying vintage can get you high-quality clothes for a fraction of the original price. Many charity shops now specialise in pulling out designer gear from their donations for particular shops.

Clothes swaps with friends and family are also a great way to spice up your wardrobe without waste. One of my sisters wears the same size as me and we swap our 'going out' dresses on a regular basis.

Another option to slow down your fashion waste is to buy quality whenever you can. I've never regretted splashing out on a (second-hand but still expensive) winter coat from a really fancy brand, which has lasted me three winters so far. Although I swallowed hard before buying it, it's one of my best ever bargain buys.

DEMAND LESS WASTE 8

We can do our best to cut plastic waste, but our efforts are constrained by the actions companies and governments take to back us up.

Give your support to campaigns calling for more taxes on wasteful packaging at its source – the manufacturer. The plastic bag tax in the UK has been a huge success, reducing the numbers given out in shops by 85 per cent. Similar measures across Europe have led to conservationists seeing a drop of nearly a third in the number of plastic bags found in our seas.

But we need more regulations that aren't just about our own consumer behaviour. The 'green dot' scheme in Germany, which makes producers buy rights for the packaging they produce according to its weight, has created a real incentive for manufacturers to cut down packaging and should be adopted by more countries.

You can ask for action directly, too. If a favourite product of yours has too much packaging, why not write to the firm responsible and point out how it is affecting your loyalty to them? Companies are sometimes more likely to listen carefully to one committed customer taking the time to write in than to a group of protestors with a banner outside their headquarters!

9 CLOSE THE LOOP

Of course, sending things for recycling is fine, but where do things go after that?

Recycling can save a lot of energy that's used in making new materials, particularly products made of glass and metal. Making products from recycled aluminium uses just one twentieth of the energy needed to make them from scratch.

More products than you might think are already being made from recycled materials. Green bottles made in the UK consist of 85 per cent recycled glass. The printers I use for Green Party materials print on recycled paper for all their customers, which is just as high quality as new stock, and most newspapers and almost all cardboard boxes are made from a high proportion of recycled paper pulp.

But materials can only be re-used if there's a demand for them, and most of the demand for plastic is currently with manufacturers in East Asia – a long way from your local recycling centre.

You can help by buying things made from recycled plastic, and asking manufacturers of your favourite products to switch to recycled material for their bottles and packets too.

Make the effort to seek out the very wide range of recycled plastic items now being produced closer to home, including pencils, flooring, fencing, water butts, window frames, files and folders, furniture, clothing, shoes, toys, sunglasses, reusable coffee mugs, shopping bags, kitchen utensils, rugs and even skateboards.

One tonne of plastic that's re-used in this way saves more than 16 barrels of oil, and needs about 60 per cent less energy than new 'virgin' plastic. It also prevents a huge amount of material going to landfill and potentially out to sea, so the more we can close the loop this way, the more we can help protect our environment and wildlife.

10 GREENER CELEBRATIONS

Birthdays, weddings and holiday seasons are full of traditions that don't have to be wasteful to be fun and special. For your parties and celebrations, try these tips to reduce your impact on the planet.

Catering for larger numbers doesn't have to mean a sea of 'disposable' plastic plates, cups, straws and cutlery. Greener alternatives are out there, made of paper, wood, bamboo or even pressed leaves.

Try to steer clear of balloons and plastic decorations. Opt for paper or cloth bunting instead, or make your own from recycled materials.

Please never release balloons into the sky, as they can cause huge damage to wildlife. Floating or flying lanterns are even worse, and can cause wildfires and harm to birds and animals.

There are many firms making delicious ethical, fair trade chocolate and drinks ideal for celebrations. And a special dinner is the perfect excuse for getting high welfare organic meat and cooking locally sourced vegetables.

Children's birthdays deserve special parties and days out, which can be very green. Many nature reserves and outdoor education organisations offer group bookings for children to enjoy messy, fun activities outdoors like woodland games and pond-dipping.

When choosing a present, try to avoid increasing the amount of stuff in the world by giving non-material gifts. Vouchers and tickets for arts and cultural events, donations to projects that support wildlife and memberships for charitable organisations are some of the nicest things I've received and were really appreciated.

If you're putting together a wedding list, there are great green products at a range of prices to ask for, and many couples now let people donate to charity in their name as an alternative option.

For other wedding essentials, look out for vintage or recycled fabric wedding dresses as a beautiful and timeless alternative. Green jewellers are increasing in number too, so seek one out for your wedding rings. These use only recycled metals, avoiding the huge impact gold mining has on soil and water pollution. And it's really important to make sure any diamonds are not being mined to support conflicts around the world. The Kimberley Process Certification Scheme helps you avoid this ethical pitfall.

GREENER BABIES

The world has thankfully now caught up with the need to protect young babies from toxic chemicals and potentially unsafe ingredients in food, clothes and toys. Now almost all pre-prepared baby food is free from preservatives, colours and artificial ingredients, and organic options are easy to find.

Every packaged baby meal still builds up in your recycling bin though, so why not whizz homemade meals up in batches and store them in the freezer in your own re-usable containers to save waste and money?

Babies also go through a lot of gadgets, clothes and toys they grow out of quickly. Use free services like your local library to find baby books and toys, and make sure friends and family know you are happy to use things their own children have finished with. I'm very proud of the hand-me-down 1970s clothes I'm wearing in the photos of me as a toddler, including a flared boiler suit I wore as much as I could!

The highest impact your baby will have in the early years is through their nappies. 'Real' or washable nappies have come on hugely in recent years and you can save water, energy and plenty of cash by using them whenever you can. You can usually get advice and help with the initial expense from your local council and women's groups.

ENERGY

Overall, around 30 per cent of our climate change emissions come from our homes, but we could reduce these hugely with a few simple energy-saving measures, and by choosing greener ways to get the remaining energy we need.

We'll start this section with draughts and insulation, because the best kind of heating is heating you don't have to do, because you have a home that keeps in the warmth rather than letting it out to heat up your street.

About three quarters of your heating energy will be squandered through your roof, windows, walls and doors if you have a poorly insulated, draughty home. Many of the measures you can take to cut down on this waste cost very little and pay back quickly in reduced bills.

Other savings can be achieved at low cost just by changing how you use your home and how you buy your energy, while others are more of an investment that takes longer to pay back. But remember that you'll be enjoying a cosier home and helping the planet all through this time, and these tips will all pay you back in the end.

12 DRAUGHTPROOF YOUR HOME

This is the simplest and cheapest way to make your home warmer, greener and less costly to heat. In an old home, a large proportion of heat loss can be due to draughts, so fixing these can be a really easy way to cut your losses.

Putting draughtproofing strips around your windows is a simple task that you can do yourself in a few hours. These are generally made of self-adhesive foam or rubber-like material that squashes and creates a seal when the window is shut.

Don't forget to deal with the draughts from doors as well. Front doors should have an insulating brush over the letterbox, and all exterior doors should have a brush strip fitted around the bottom.

For an extra layer of draughtproofing, why not hang a curtain in front of an exterior door? Regardless of climate considerations, this can make your hallway feel and look cosier during the winter months.

Other places where draughts may lurk are in the loft and where pipes lead to the outside. A professional draughtproofing firm can help fill these gaps for you at a low cost that will make your home really cosy. They will also be able to check you have the right level of ventilation in rooms that need it, like bathrooms and kitchens.

Improving windows with secondary glazing or new double-glazed units is another major improvement you can make. Even if you have an older house with heritage windows, there are specialist firms that can make double-glazed replacements to match. Look for the energy rating of any new window you choose. A++ is currently the highest rating, and you can find these in all kinds of materials, including wood. And don't forget that efficient windows will also keep your house quieter by keeping out noise from outside, in addition to the cold air.

13 INSULATE YOUR HOME

A quarter of your energy can be lost through an uninsulated loft. If you've neglected this job or have older, thinner insulation (at least 270mm (10½ inches) is the minimum recommended now), this is where to start.

Laying down insulation rolls, between and then across the ceiling joists, is a DIY job that most people can do. The most common material is mineral wool, but there are greener options that take less energy to produce, including sheep's wool, hemp and flax.

Your walls can be responsible for another third of your heat loss. You may have cavity walls (two layers of bricks with a gap between) or solid walls (a thicker, single layer of bricks) and the solutions are different for each.

For cavity walls, professional engineers simply drill a hole in the wall and pump in material to fill the gap to prevent heat passing through. This is a very good value way to save a lot of energy. Older, solid wall homes are more complicated and more expensive to insulate, but there can be grants available to help.

Solid wall homes need either external insulation, which puts a thin layer of insulating material on the outside, or internal insulation, which adds a layer of insulation to all the walls that face the outside.

USE THE SUN'S HEAT | 14

The most energy efficient homes are known as 'passive houses' (invented in Germany, the standard is called Passivhaus). These are designed with high thermal efficiency and are virtually airtight, with ventilation that circulates and recaptures heat.

Almost the only heating in a passive house comes from the sun, with strategically placed windows designed to capture the sun's energy. They have more windows in south-facing walls (in the northern hemisphere at least) and fewer, smaller windows to the north. This makes sure morning heat is captured to the fullest, and prevents heat escaping on the colder side of the house.

In an existing home, you can use some of the same principles to make the most of the sun's heat.

In colder months, make sure that south-facing windows have their shades open in the morning, and capture more heat by having dark walls and flooring materials in these areas. Conversely, to prevent overheating from south-facing windows in summer, keep these shades closed through the morning instead. A clever way to seasonally adjust your solar gain is to plant deciduous trees and shrubs outside south-facing windows. In winter, their bare branches will let the sun's heat through, and they will act as a useful shade in summer.

To cool your home on hot days, use strategic window opening. Create a current through the house by opening windows both upstairs and downstairs.

LOW CARBON HEATING 5

Heating accounts for more than half the cost of energy used by the average home. So let's start with an easy way to cut down your costs by turning down the heat.

Many homes are set at a temperature that's just a bit too high, and reducing your thermostat setting by one degree can save you ten per cent on your heating bill. Nineteen degrees is plenty unless you are older or moving around very little, and don't forget to set the timer so that the heating doesn't come on when you're out at work.

A great way to save is with a smart meter – this shows you what you're using, and lets you experiment with different appliances and heat settings to see the impact on your costs.

If you're refurbishing a home, explore options for lower carbon heating and hot water. There are a lot of choices and good advice available on what will work for you.

Even if you aren't planning a major change, replacing an older gas boiler with an efficient A-rated model can save a lot on your heating bills, making it a very worthwhile investment. If you don't have a gas supply to your home, you should also explore lower carbon options, like heat pumps and biomass boilers.

16 SEE THE LIGHT

If you've ever tried to change a traditional lightbulb soon after it has been switched off, you'll know that, as well as light, these inefficient dinosaurs also give off a lot of heat. These days, we have much more clever ways of producing light from electricity.

Fluorescent bulbs work by using electrical charges to make a white coating on the inside of the glass glow brightly. They are so much more efficient than traditional bulbs – and last so much longer – that each one will save you much more than it costs in electricity bills and replacements over its lifetime. If you have any incandescent lamps left in your home, switch them now.

A more recent innovation is the light-emitting diode (LED). This is a very simple electronic component that almost never breaks, and converts electricity directly into light. LEDs are extremely energy efficient and last ten times longer than even fluorescent bulbs. You can now get LED lamps to fit in traditional light sockets and to replace the very energy-hungry halogen spotlights in your ceiling.

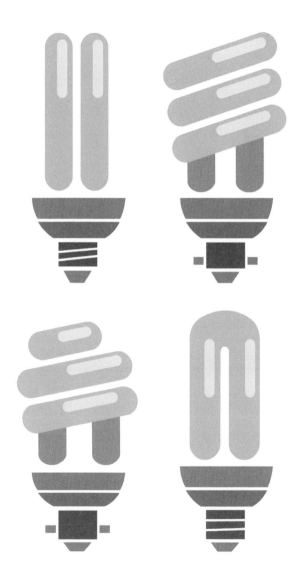

17 GREEN MACHINES

Choosing the best household appliances and using the machines you own wisely can make a massive difference to your energy use. We have many more machines in our homes than we used to – in fact the amount of electricity consumed by the average home has increased 40 per cent since the 1970s.

These days, modern energy labels make choosing the best appliances easier, and the standards are going up constantly. Look for the highest rating – up to A+++ nowadays – and be careful to choose the right size appliance for you. Even with a high energy rating a larger machine will use more energy.

Electronics are a big drain on energy, too. Unlike white goods, newer plasma televisions use more energy than their older counterparts. Liquid crystal or LED TVs are more energy-efficient. And laptops use much less energy than desktop computers.

A constant frustration of mine is machines without a proper 'off' switch, meaning they sit on standby power all the time. While this isn't always high, it can add up, so look for machines that have high energy ratings and low standby power consumption, and always turn things like printers and games consoles off at the plug whenever you can.

DIVEST 18

The green movement knows that we need to be leaving most of the remaining coal, oil and gas in the ground if we're going to prevent the earth tipping over into disastrous climate change.

The logic follows that companies which extract fossil fuels, whose value depends on assumptions about extracting and selling their reserves, aren't going to be good investments in the long term. Activists in the global divestment movement are campaigning for big pension funds and public investments to stop holding stocks and shares in these companies, and move their money to more futureproof industries.

They have won some victories, with some cities, universities and other public pension funds now making plans to stop fossil fuel investment. The pressure to change is coming from workers, citizens and customers. So, if your pension fund is still counting on fossil fuels to provide for your future, you can help change this.

If you have a personal pension there are now many choices of investment funds offering the choice to be ethical and fossil-free, so ask your financial advisor to investigate. If you have a company or institutional pension, why not gather other pension holders together and ask divestment campaigners to help you work for a switch to a greener future?

19 BUY GREENER ENERGY

Our electricity supply is responsible for a quarter of greenhouse gas emissions in the UK. You can help increase investment in new wind, solar, wave and tidal energy by opting to pay for greener electricity through your energy supplier.

Greener tariffs can make a real difference. However, it's important that they don't just allocate renewable energy being generated anyway to certain customers. The 'big six' energy suppliers have largely given up on green tariffs, but a number of smaller companies offer good deals.

If you opt for a greener tariff, it needs to create new capacity and new investment in renewable energy. The Ethical Consumer website rates green electricity tariffs according to a range of criteria, including their tax-paying policies, and is the best way to compare what will do the most good. Other consumer switching sites also compare the deals, and have found that a fixed-rate deal from a green supplier is often cheaper than a standard variable tariff from a regular company.

You can also opt for a greener gas tariff these days, though these are just starting out. The company I use makes a proportion of its gas purchases from suppliers making household gas from bio-methane, generated from food, plant and animal waste.

GENERATE YOUR OWN 20

Both large- and small-scale projects will be needed to help the shift to green energy. By investing in green energy at home, or as part of a community project, you can reduce your bills, help support a new industry and cut your contribution to climate change.

Renewable energy that works at a domestic scale includes solar electricity, solar hot water, small wind turbines, wood-pellet boilers (not so good in urban areas with air pollution problems) and air- and ground-source heat pumps. The best option for you will depend on where you live, the space you have and the structure of your home, so do get expert advice.

An initial consultation is often free, and grants to help install renewable energy at home may also be available, though they are usually in short supply. In the UK, the Energy Saving Trust can help find expert advice and any available grants.

I've recently backed my local community energy enterprise: Power Up North London. They are putting solar panels on local churches and community buildings to help save energy for these vital institutions, while also generating a small return for investors. Many more of these groups are springing up all over the country, so seek out one near you and help them grow.

21 | SAVE WATER IN THE HOME

Having fresh water on tap is so convenient we don't often think about saving it. But, with more of us moving to a metered supply where every litre is paid for, and with climate change leading to more droughts and shortages, we should all be more careful about the water we use. Here are a few top tips for saving water around the home.

Choose and use appliances well – Washing machines and dishwashers have eco-labels that show how much water they use, as well as energy, so make sure to choose an efficient model. And always run a full load to get the most out of your machines. With a washing machine this means really filling up the drum and not leaving lots of space.

Save when you flush – Flushing the toilet is responsible for about 30 per cent of all the water we use in the home. Older models can use up to 13 litres per flush, compared with less than six for modern loos. These should always be fitted with a water saving 'hippo' inside to cut this down. Newer toilets with dual flush options are helpful too, and don't forget the 'deep green' option of not flushing every time – if you live on your own you can save a lot of water and not lose any friends!

Switch your taps and shower heads – As well as fixing any drips (which can really add up – one drip per second can produce more than 15,000 litres going to waste in a year), fit aerating tap and shower fittings, which mix air with water to give the feeling and appearance of quite high flow rates with lower water usage.

See tip 45 (Use Water Wisely) for how to save water in the garden.

22 MEND IT!

Repairing and refurbishing things is one of my favourite activities – partly for green reasons but also because working with my hands to solve problems is a really good way to take a break from typing emails on a computer, which most of my work consists of.

We are turning into a throwaway society. Over six million electrical items are thrown away every year in the UK alone. This is a waste of materials if they aren't all recycled, and also a waste of the energy used to make them.

Many things don't need to be thrown away at all, but could be repaired to last several years more. One way to help cut waste is to choose items that are designed to be longer lasting and repairable. This can make things more expensive at first but, if you find yourself throwing away a cheap toaster every year, will prove a good investment in the end.

Some simple repairs you can do yourself. Get to grips with how to change a fuse, look for simple loose screws and broken connections if a machine stops working suddenly, and use a superglue or epoxy resin to fix snapped off knobs, levers and handles. Many components are designed to be replaced every so often, such as fan belts, filters and heating elements, and you can find instructions in the manual or on the internet for how to order and replace these.

Another thing to do is use any remaining skilled repair people in your local area. Many independent electrical shops still offer good-value repair services, and supporting local businesses is also great for the local economy.

One of my best investments is a sewing machine, and sewing by hand is also a good skill to develop. Knowing how to sew on buttons, repair hems, sew patches and ripped pockets, and even adjust second-hand clothes to fit properly is great. You can find many online video tutorials to show you the basics of sewing, helping your clothes to last longer and look better.

23 RECLAIM AND REFURBISH

Re-use is one of the green 'three Rs'. Buying things second-hand is a very good way to make the earth's resources go further, and also get a bargain in the process.

The internet has taken over from newspaper classified ads as the best place to find and sell used items, and there's almost nothing you can't find online. There are also local networks for 'freecycling' items, and these are worth a look at if you're setting up a home or office and want quality items for less.

A bit of work can make even battered items like new again. I have a lot of second-hand 20th Century furniture. With some sanding and oiling or a lick of new paint, tables, chests and dining chairs (with new seat pads and covers added) can be made like new again.

People also dump reclaimable items into skips and on the street. This fly-tipping is not allowed, but I made a lovely side table from the legs of a tubular steel stool that I found in a local hotspot.

Even if you're not very hands-on, these spruce ups are not much more trouble than following the assembly instructions on a flat-pack item, and there are good books available to show you how to do it well.

TRAVEL

The travel choices we make have a big impact on the contribution we make to climate change, but our governments and city planners don't always make it easy to do things better. It has taken far too long for greener vehicles to start to become normal, and poor regulation and delays in getting basics like electric charging points on our streets are to blame.

I want to put our travel choices in context. We do have alternatives for many of the short journeys we make by car, and if we think more about each journey we will find we can cut down and combine trips to save time as well as carbon, while getting the same amount done. Reducing the amount of traffic on our streets isn't just a good thing to do because of carbon emissions. Air pollution grows alongside all kinds of motor travel, and fewer vehicles clogging up our roads also makes them safer and nicer for people, helping children to play and local shops and businesses to thrive on healthier streets.

For longer trips and holidays the growth in air travel is a real threat to achieving our carbon targets so, in this section, you can also read about the joys of holidaying closer to home and exploring the world in different ways.

24 WALKING BACK TO HAPPINESS

People are walking less than in earlier decades, and this affects our wellbeing in many different ways.

To be fit and healthy we should be physically active, but most of us don't move around nearly enough. Only about one in 20 people in England are active enough for good health, and it's been estimated that, on current trends, the average British citizen will only be using 25 per cent more energy on a daily basis than if they spent the whole time sleeping!

Walking is a proven treatment for stress and helps to improve mental wellbeing in people who take regular longer walks. Many great writers, including Charles Dickens, Beatrix Potter and William Wordsworth, did a lot of their thinking while taking walks. Even if you're not planning to create works of art, walking is good for you. People who walk on the way to work or go for a stroll at lunchtime report that they feel more alert and think more clearly as a result.

A quarter of all car trips cover distances that could be walked instead. There is a lot of talk about the problem of obesity, and you'd be forgiven for thinking this was all down to eating more, but the reduction in active travel has made a real difference.

Walking is a great way to keep at a healthy weight. Studies in the USA have shown that each extra kilometre walked per day leads to around a five per cent reduction in the chances of becoming obese, whereas each extra hour spent in the car per day increases this risk by about six per cent.

The key to walking more is to make it second nature rather than an 'extra' thing that you might give up after a few tries. So, build walking into your daily journey into work or change how you shop as an ideal way to increase your number of walking steps. Why not get off the bus a stop earlier, or walk to the railway station from home instead of getting a lift? If your journey to work is only a few kilometres by car, you could even walk the whole way a couple of times a week to cut down on traffic as well as your stress (and this is an ideal trip to take by bike, too).

Shopping locally can cut down on car journeys and support local businesses. Instead of getting all your groceries on a big trip to the supermarket, try switching to more 'top up shopping', walking home from the station in the evening via local shops to pick up just what you need for a couple of days at a time.

While at work, you can also be more active by climbing the stairs instead of taking the lift when you're only going a few floors up. This everyday activity raises your heart rate and breathing enough to count as real exercise, keeping you fitter without a special trip to the gym.

25 WALK TO SCHOOL

I walked to my primary school every day and was allowed to do this without my mum, with a friend from next door, from the age of seven. Hardly anyone drove to school, so I was shocked when I found out that now only half of young children walk to school and around 40 per cent are taken by car.

Start creating confident, streetwise kids by walking with them to school when they are small. Make the journey fun and use it to get to know your local area. After walking with you for years, they should be well equipped to walk on their own when they get bigger, and take no risks with strangers or traffic.

Many parents' groups and schools are now setting up 'walking buses'. These involve two or three parents supervising up to 20 children, who walk together on a route via each of their homes and then on to school. This helps parents save time when it's not their turn to supervise and builds up children's confidence out on the streets. Talk to other parents and get advice from the local council and walking charities to see if your school could do this too.

26 BIKE TO WORK, SCHOOL, THE SHOPS AND TO HEALTH

Did you know that the bicycle is the most energy-efficient way of getting around? It even beats walking as the lowest energy user per kilometre, because of the way its clever system of wheels, pedals and gears converts human energy to transport.

Cities that make cycling easier see the benefits for their citizens in terms of less traffic and pollution, healthier streets and healthier citizens. People worry about their safety on a bike, and we do need many more protected separate cycle lanes to attract more people to riding bikes at all ages. However, cycling is still a safe way to get around, and the health benefits mean life expectancy for regular cyclists goes up overall.

Cycle to save time

With traffic in cities still grinding along at the average speed of a horse and carriage thanks to congestion, cycling can be the quickest way to commute. Because you spend most of your journey on the move, and because it's a door-to-door journey, cycling is the fastest way to make a short urban journey at busy times. Another good thing is its predictability. Unlike motor travel at the mercy of jams and delays, bike trips take almost exactly the same amount of time every day, increasing your reliability and reducing your stress.

If you're not ready to commute to work every day by bike, or your journey is too long, start by replacing some of your journeys with a bike ride.

To the shops
Get a basket or pannier and cycle to your local shops to combine all the benefits of fitness, cutting pollution, cutting down on waste and supporting your local economy.

To the train
Any journey of a few kilometres is an ideal bike journey. If you are commuting by car because the station is too far away, taking the bike to the train can be the perfect combination. Lots of trains will take full-size bikes, but the best bikes to use in combination with public transport are compact folding models. I have one of these and it's really flexible. I can also take it into pubs and people's houses without worrying about leaving it in the street.

27 SHARE A LIFT

Another very simple way to cut your emissions is to share a lift with someone else who is going to the same place. You'd probably be delighted if you could achieve twice the fuel efficiency without spending money on a new car, but by sharing regular journeys with others, you can already cut your per-person emissions and fuel use in half.

A lot of the congestion and parking problems around major events like football matches, festivals and concerts could be reduced if people going there shared their cars with each other. Organising lift sharing to events you're attending with friends is as easy as making a phone call. A good way to find travel buddies you don't already know for big events is to use a service such as the Liftshare website. This helps people find travelling companions for regular trips and major journeys.

Liftshare also helps companies with travel planning and getting employees to share lifts to work. Commuters in cars are much more likely to be travelling alone compared with the average driver, so the workplace is the ideal location for organising car sharing among people who live near each other and travel to the same place every day.

28 PLAN YOUR TRIPS

Do you ever have days when you feel like a one-person taxi service? You get home from a trip to the shops, then immediately have to ferry the kids to a football practice they didn't warn you about, and when you get home again there's a phone call asking you to take something to grandma's house.

Having a car in the driveway ready to use whenever you want can make taking extra trips a little bit too convenient, leading to demand for more car journeys than you would take if it was more expensive or difficult to arrange.

So, one very effective way to save on car travel is to plan your trips more in advance and combine more trips into one. All of the three separate journeys in my example above could have been combined into one round trip, saving dramatically on fuel, carbon emissions, and your time spent driving around.

If you don't travel by car, then journey planning is already a habit you probably have. Smart phones now make it even easier to plan ahead, use public transport and avoid getting taxis due to running out of time. Get an app to help you plan the most efficient ways to get where you want and keep on top of any delays at the same time.

DATA IN GRAMS/OUNCES OF CARBON DIOXIDE, PER KILOMETRE, PER PASSENGER

Diesel coach (average occupancy):
28g (1 oz)

Average car (medium-sized, four people):
43g (1½ oz)

Train:
47g (>1½ oz)

Diesel London Bus (average occupancy):
 73g (2½ oz)

Average car (medium-sized, one person):
173g (6 oz)

Plane (average occupancy):
160–270g
(5½ – 9½ oz)

LOWER CARBON TRAVEL

29

When deciding how to travel it helps to know the impact you're having. While there are lots of other effects on the environment, the impact on climate change is useful to compare ways of getting around so I've looked up what this is for typical vehicles today.

Active travel – walking and cycling using human power – is almost carbon neutral per kilometre, except for the food needed to give you energy. The carbon cost of other modes of transport depends a lot on how many people each vehicle is carrying.

Buses have big engines, and there are lots of air pollution emissions from diesel engines that mean cleaner buses are a big priority for cities. But everyone who takes the bus helps the planet. It's taking the route anyway, so everyone on board is saving all the carbon they would have burned if they had jumped in the car instead. As well as filling up the bus, filling up your car by sharing lifts on regular journeys is also a good way to reduce your impact.

For longer distance travel, coaches have the lowest impact. Trains are switching to electricity and lowering the average carbon footprint too. But planes are very carbon hungry so, even in a full plane, your impact from taking a flight remains very high indeed.

GREENER VEHICLES 30

When walking, cycling and public transport can't cover every regular journey you need to make, a vehicle for personal travel may be essential. But this doesn't have to mean owning a car: in most cities you could join one of the growing number of car clubs.

Signing up to a car club lets you pay by the hour and drive when you really need to, but without the upfront costs and hassle of owning a car. Car club members who drive less than 6000–8000 miles can save several thousand pounds.

Alternatively, an electric powered bicycle makes longer journeys by bike (and uphill ones!) much easier. A motorbike or scooter is also worth considering. They take up much less space, are easier to park and get good mileage on a lower carbon footprint.

We are at last seeing electric and plug-in hybrid cars at much more affordable prices, and with grants available to help buy them. They are gaining fast in popularity, with 150,000 plug-in vehicles now on the road in the UK, compared with just 3,500 in 2013. On average they can drive more than 200 miles on a single charge without using any fossil fuels directly (though of course the full carbon impact also includes whatever generates the electricity).

3 WORK MORE FROM HOME

Only one in 15 people works at home regularly, but many more of us could work at least some of the time away from the office if we asked for more flexibility.

For the planet, the main benefits of home-working come through avoiding the impact of our trips to work. Since slow, congested traffic creates higher carbon emissions per mile, the savings from people spending just one day at home every fortnight could cut rush hour traffic by ten per cent, and carbon emissions by even more.

There are other benefits from staying at home to work some of the time. Away from the chatter of colleagues, it can be easier to work on a project that needs concentrated attention. Staying at home can be better for work-life balance too: you can spend your lunch hour catching up on housework and be at home when the children get back from school.

32 WHAT THE BOSS CAN DO

Transport to work and as part of our jobs has a huge impact on the world. Could your company get better at video conferencing to cut down on flights and carbon? Are your polluting diesel delivery vans in need of being replaced by (cheaper to run) electric vehicles? What changes could save money, not just the environment?

You can probably make the most difference by asking your boss to look at these issues across the board and develop a workplace travel plan.

This will look at how employees get to work, how customers reach you, and how deliveries are organised and transported, and a good travel plan will also involve employees in thinking about ideas for how to change things.

Measures that most workplaces could take include switching more quickly to the cleanest fleet vehicles, and helping people with incentives like the tax breaks available to buy a bike to use to cycle to work. Asking for or subsidising better local transport services where they are needed is also an option for larger workplaces.

And companies with car parks can encourage people to car-share by allocating free parking spaces to those who share lifts.

33 HOLIDAY NEARER HOME

We've all been sold the same image of the 'ideal holiday' – a palm tree and a stretch of white sand next to a turquoise sea. But is that really what makes for a perfect break? Does going far away guarantee having a relaxing time, and does a few days of tropical weather make up for the hassle of negotiating airports and long flights?

For most people, spending quality time with their families or friends is what they want from a break. Interesting activities, great food and comfortable places to stay don't have to mean getting on a plane. In fact, most of us can find ideal holiday spots closer to home. For me, the UK has everything I need for most of my breaks, from a fantastic range of coastlines, to hills and mountains that are just the right height to hike up for a brilliant view, without needing climbing gear.

In the UK we have history to spare, with more World Heritage Sites than the whole of the USA, from Stonehenge to the castles of North Wales and the Roman city of Bath. We also have amazing food in our seaside towns, and the best local pubs, while more and more companies are offering adventure and activity breaks ideal for families.

If you're not from the UK, don't be envious. Your own close-to-home breaks will offer a similar range of things to explore. The principle of prioritising what you do, not how far you travel, helps you get to know your own backyard and enjoy more holidays that relax, inform and entertain you without breaking the carbon bank.

34 SEEING THE WORLD

When you want to travel further afield for a holiday to explore other places and cultures, travelling by air is the most carbon-heavy option of all, but there are plenty of alternatives for how to get there. Many make for a more satisfying trip, not just one that impacts the earth less.

Some of the most renowned romantic journeys are by rail. But you don't have to travel on the Orient Express to make the most of the romance of travelling by train. Long-distance, inter-city trains with sleeper cars and restaurants can get you all over Europe and beyond, as well as taking you between cities in the USA and Asia. Good travel agents and online booking services can find you the right connections and book your trains and hotels at the same time. See pages 108–110 for how to find them.

Sea travel doesn't lack romance either. Unfortunately, large cruise ships can be as carbon-intensive as planes per passenger kilometre (although since you also live on board, this includes your accommodation). For shorter trips, ferries can save carbon compared with planes. This varies with different ship types though: a super-fast ferry or catamaran can have as much impact as flying.

A holiday by car can also be a good choice. Four people with luggage in the average car will burn less carbon than a plane and, by taking the car, your holiday starts as soon as you leave home. You can take your car on ferries around the Channel, North Sea, Baltic and Mediterranean, and in Europe there are some Motorail services where you can put your car on the back of a train and relax on the way.

35 TO OFFSET OR NOT?

Carbon offsetting may have seemed like a perfect solution to a high-carbon activity like flying, but it has proved very complicated to get right. There are three major problems with the concept of flying now and paying for someone else to 'offset' your emissions later.

1. The savings might not happen or may take too long

When you fly, the emissions go right into the atmosphere straight away, while offsetting projects that do things like plant trees tend to count the carbon saved over many decades. There's no real guarantee that all the projects started will last that long, but all the damage from your plane trip is there in the meantime.

Offsetting companies have also got into difficulties with schemes that aim to make savings through development projects in poorer countries, which take too long to get going, or fail to happen at all.

2. The savings could have happened anyway

Offsetting schemes sometimes struggle to prove their savings are really new reductions to count against your flight.

Many countries are adopting more cost-effective green technologies anyway as they develop, rather than the polluting industries of the past. In many cases, it's hard to be sure that a project paid for by offsetting would not have found some other way to get going.

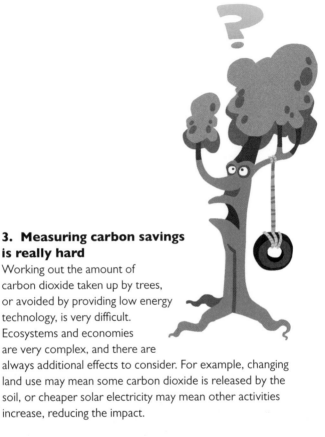

3. Measuring carbon savings is really hard

Working out the amount of carbon dioxide taken up by trees, or avoided by providing low energy technology, is very difficult. Ecosystems and economies are very complex, and there are always additional effects to consider. For example, changing land use may mean some carbon dioxide is released by the soil, or cheaper solar electricity may mean other activities increase, reducing the impact.

Now, don't get me wrong. There are many good environmental projects that I would massively encourage you to donate to, and a very good time to do it is when you're concerned about the impact of a flight you are taking – in fact you should give as much as you can at these times.

However, thinking of the money you give as actually cancelling out the carbon from your flight is a mistake, and not a good reason to fly more than you have to.

COOKING
& EATING

The amount of resources that goes into what we eat isn't just reflected on our plates. Food miles, water usage, food that's wasted before it even gets to the shops, and unsustainable farming practices all add to the impact of keeping ourselves well fed and healthy.

A lot of the international food trade has more to do with commerce than necessity. Some things can only be grown in certain places, and the long distance transport of goods like spices, coffee, cocoa, tea and fruit goes back centuries, but many things are traded back and forth without much rationality, in what green campaigners have called 'the great food swap'.

Big multinational companies are mainly responsible, as they can cope with larger transport costs to chase cheaper materials and labour, but there are also some international trade agreements that actually put up barriers to things like local councils choosing local suppliers for their food.

It's part of my job as a Green Party campaigner to work for better trade rules and higher ethical and green standards for our food. Meanwhile, you can make a difference, and save money at the same time, with these pieces of advice for your daily life.

36 DON'T WASTE GOOD FOOD

In richer countries, far too much of our food goes to waste. My mum used to get me to finish my plate by telling me how lucky I was compared to many children, and now climate change is making food insecurity even worse for people around the world.

This makes it very important not just to buy food with a lower carbon footprint but also not to waste the food we buy. In terms of its impact, reducing food waste could do almost as much good as making the effort to eat more eco-friendly foods.

We waste more than we think

Around half the food waste in the UK occurs in the home – far more than in farms, factories or restaurants. A research project in England asked people to keep a diary of what they put in the bin. The total – including vegetable peelings, bones, spoiled food from the fridge, rotten fruit, stale bread and many other things – was more than a third of all the food they bought.

At least half of our wasted food could have been eaten if it had been managed better. And the cost of all the food we throw away in a lifetime could add up to a year's salary!

Why are we throwing away so much food?

One of the major reasons is unplanned large shopping trips. If we do a big shop without making a list and checking our cupboards first, some of what we buy will inevitably end up going bad before it is used.

We are also easily tempted by special 'buy one get one free' offers. And once we get our food home, we're also not very good at storing perishable foods or using the oldest things first.

Tips to reduce food waste

Young people and families waste the most food, but we can learn from our older generations on this. They can remember when food was scarcer and more expensive and are far more likely to shop in an organised way and cook planned meals from scratch.

You don't need to become housekeeper of the year, though. Just thinking about the problem can help us develop better habits. Try some of these tips:

• Make shopping lists and check what you have in the cupboard before setting off, to avoid buying things you already have in stock, and plan meals to use older items up.

• Buy more loose fruit and vegetables, so you buy the right amount for the recipes you are making. Salad vegetables are the most commonly wasted, so try to buy these fresh when you want them from your local shops, rather than during a weekly supermarket trip.

• Keep your fridge at the right temperature – between 2 and 4 degrees will help keep food fresher for longer – and don't leave the door open for long periods and risk things warming up.

• Look at use-by or best-before dates, and put things that need using soon near the front of fridges, freezers and cupboards, not tucked away at the back.

And don't forget, almost all food waste like peelings can be used to feed your garden if you put it in the compost – see tip 42 (Compost) for more about this.

CUT DOWN ON MEAT 37

Eating less meat is not just an ethical choice. The impact of meat production on the health of our planet is very widely appreciated nowadays, and the number of people choosing to be vegetarian or vegan is growing rapidly.

I am a very light consumer of meat, and I've also cut down on cheese recently. I often go for a whole week without any animal parts reaching my plate. And if they do, it's likely to be organic chicken, a bit of sustainably-caught fish or a slice or two of salami. I hardly ever touch red meat, and the reasons for these changes to my diet are almost completely environmental.

A lot of the problem with meat eating is the climate impact of methane, a very potent climate change gas. The digestive systems of farmed cows and sheep and other animals are estimated to be responsible for around 30 per cent of the total methane from human activity.

Rearing animals for food, calorie for calorie, also uses far more land and water than growing plant-based food. Beef has the highest impact of all, needing 28 times more land and 11 times more water than the average of a range of different foods analysed in a recent study.

When you think about how we're growing good crops only to feed to animals we raise to eat, the efficiency of eating more vegetarian food is very obvious.

Think more veggie

A lot of vegetarian food is also healthier. If you want to watch fat or cholesterol, or if you're looking for extra vitamins, eating more vegetables makes so much sense. Every meal you eat without meat will also help to reduce climate change, and to preserve water and land.

Getting your workplace to do 'meat-free Mondays', choosing less meat in restaurants, and shifting more of your daily meals away from meat is simple and makes a real difference, even if you don't want to go full vegetarian.

Try new ingredients and recipes

I was sceptical about two vegetarian protein staples – tofu and lentils – until I tried them properly. They are both delicious and easy to cook. Tofu is perfect for a stir fry. Just marinate it in soy sauce and plenty of garlic and ginger and throw it in the wok to brown before adding your favourite vegetables and sauce.

Lentil soup is fine, but my two favourite recipes with lentils are spicy dhal, made with red lentils mixed with fried onions, garlic, fresh chillies and spices, and a warm French salad made with green lentils and steamed green vegetables drenched in a vinaigrette dressing.

A mixture of beans, peppers and tomatoes with smoked chilli powder also makes a fantastic meat-free filling for tacos. Dried beans and pulses aren't just healthy and full of fibre, they are really cheap too. Simply soak them overnight before you want to use them.

• For more ideas, see the Vegetarian Society's website, which also has advice on a balanced diet: www.vegsoc.org

• The Vegan Society has many recipes for meals which also avoid dairy and other animal products: www.vegansociety.com

• The BBC's Food website has thousands of recipes that are easy to search for vegetarian options: www.bbc.com/food

38 EAT LOCAL AND ORGANIC

About a third of all goods transported in lorries on our roads each year are farming and food products, and about ten per cent of the total carbon footprint of our food is due to the distance it travels to our plates.

Help cut your food miles by eating more seasonal food: root vegetables instead of salads in the winter, and locally grown fruit when it's in abundance in the summer and autumn.

Organic farmers use less energy to produce food than conventional farming, and work hard to preserve wildlife, water and soil health. Healthy soils also help store carbon from the atmosphere. Organic meat also has very high welfare standards for animals so, wherever you can, choosing certified organic food will help the planet and its creatures a lot.

Food from farmers' markets and organic box schemes isn't cheap but is healthy and low impact and helps your local economy as a whole more than big supermarkets. My local green shops all sell loose produce so you can buy only as much as you need, which can help save money too.

Go for imported produce that travels by ship, not plane, like fair trade and organic bananas and citrus fruits that are rarely air-freighted.

LOW-ENERGY COOKING 39

If you've ever cooked on a camping trip, you'll know that out on a windy hillside, you'd never dream of wasting heat by leaving the lid off a pan, or boiling more water than you need. But these are common ways to waste energy while cooking at home.

There's plenty of scope for applying campsite principles in our kitchens.

• Always use the right size pan for your food, and the right size ring or burner.

• Don't overfill pans with water. Just enough to cover the food is usually fine, and use a lid to stop evaporation.

• Boil water for cooking in the kettle, rather than heating it up in the pan. Kettles are more efficient as long as you only boil what you need. Don't do this when boiling eggs though, as the sudden heat will crack them!

• Pasta will cook in more or less the same time without being held at the boil. Turn off the heat once the cooking water boils, and put on a tight-fitting lid. Come back after the normal cooking time, and you should find it's ready to eat.

40 COOL DOWN YOUR FRIDGE

Next to heating up your home, keeping perishables cold and fresh is one of the most energy-intensive activities in our houses and apartments.

You can really turn your fridge into an energy hog by leaving the door open. Try to get into the habit of thinking about what you want from the fridge before opening the door, rather than doing your meal planning while the fridge motor goes into overdrive.

Get the best energy-rated fridge you can find, make sure it's no bigger than you need, and try these other tips.

• Choose a place for your fridge that's as far away from your boiler and your cooker as possible. In a warm place, the fridge will have to work harder than necessary, which is why many people put their freezer in a cellar or garage, away from the warmth of the main home.

• Keep freezers as full as possible, but empty the fridge of old items regularly. These tips both help to reduce the energy needed to keep things at the right temperature.

• Never put warm items into the fridge or freezer. Wait for cooked food to cool down to room temperature first.

• Defrost fridges and freezers regularly, especially if your fridge has an ice compartment.

• Remove dust regularly from any exposed condenser coils at the back, so they can more easily radiate the heat away from the appliance.

• Check your door seals – a piece of paper should stay stuck in the seal even if tugged gently. If you have an appliance that regularly ices up, the seals may well be at fault, and be costing you much more than replacing them. See the manual for how to order and replace the seals on your model (and check the internet if you have lost your manual, as most are available online).

IN THE GARDEN

Gardens should be simple to keep green, and can be a really good way to support local wildlife, help absorb rainwater and combat flooding, as well as a place to grow food you can eat at its very freshest.

Paving over front gardens for driveways is a huge problem in many towns and cities, and even if you keep your garden unpaved, lawns can be a water hog sprayed with chemicals. And unless you want your garden to turn into the static equivalent of a gas-guzzler, don't even think about getting a patio heater!

The ecological sparseness of many of today's gardens, with 'untidy' hedges removed, non-native planting, lots of paving and decking has contributed to a dramatic loss of wildlife in towns and cities. Beneficial insects, including beetles and butterflies, are increasingly hard to spot, and the house sparrow is now on the Royal Society for the Protection of Birds' red list, meaning it has dramatically declined in the past 25 years.

With a small amount of work, your garden can help put some of these things right. Here are some useful tips on how to make your garden a green, low impact, wildlife-friendly haven.

41 GROW FOOD WITHOUT A GARDEN

What better way to save carbon emissions and food miles, and ensure you have fresh food you can trust, than to grow your own? Even if all you have is a few window ledges, you can still grow a range of useful crops.

Salads

Window boxes and balconies are great for easy-to-grow salad vegetables, such as rocket and lettuce. These enjoy a mixture of sun and shade, and slugs and snails will find them hard to reach.

To grow salad leaves, simply fill a window box with compost (peat-free), use a pencil to create two shallow furrows and sow your seeds along it. Cover the seeds, water gently and leave until the seedlings come up. Then, thin the rows and keep the soil just moist as the larger plants grow. When you have finished your first crop, just plant some more, or choose cut-and-come-again varieties that will grow new leaves as you pick them.

Fruit and veg

Tomatoes, potatoes and other vegetables will do well on a balcony, but need a reasonable depth of soil and some attention to watering. Grow-bags can help reduce water needs, and are great for tomatoes. They can also be re-used for other crops like salad leaves later.

Strawberries love being grown in pots and are a fantastic treat in the summer. You can even grow them in hanging baskets. Compact varieties of sweet peppers and chillies will also enjoy conditions on a sunny balcony, though netting may be needed to help protect them from wind.

Herbs

Shop-bought fresh herbs can have a huge carbon footprint, so growing your own is a way to really cut down your impact. You can grow herbs no matter how little space you have. Several kinds of herbs can be grown together in one large pot or, if you don't mind regular watering, a collection of smaller pots of herbs looks gorgeous on a window sill.

All our favourites are suitable for small pot gardens, including annuals like basil and coriander, and perennials like mint, thyme, oregano and chives.

42 COMPOST

Composting is one of the easiest and most rewarding eco-friendly activities. It saves waste and gives a useful end product, with very little time and effort. Most types of food waste can be composted down to improve the soil in your garden.

A well-tended, well-fed compost bin is teeming with life, as bugs and bacteria work to break down a wide range of organic material into a nutritious treat for your soil. You can often get a simple compost bin free from your local council, or pick one up at a garden centre.

Ingredients for a balanced diet

Feed your bin a balanced diet of organic waste, with a mixture of tough, fibrous material, softer stuff like food scraps, and 'activators' that will get things moving.

Examples of activators are:
- Grass cuttings
- Weeds
- Manure from herbivorous animals

Soft food for a nutritious mix:
- Fruit and vegetable peelings
- Used tea leaves and coffee grounds
- Vacuum cleaner dust
- Dead flowers

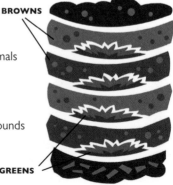

BROWNS

GREENS

Tough ingredients for body:
- Hedge clippings
- Egg shells
- Shredded cardboard
- Dead leaves

Ingredients to avoid:
- Meat and fish, and cooked food
- Newspaper in large quantities or glossy magazines
- Cat and dog waste, or nappy contents

Filling and tending your compost bin

Start filling your bin with a layer of twigs and cardboard to keep the bottom aerated. Then layer soft ingredients with tougher fibrous materials to make sure there are channels through the materials for bugs and air to circulate. It's a good idea to keep some autumn leaves or hedge clippings near your bin to keep this layering going when you add softer ingredients.

The composting process will take several months. Keep adding material, and after this time you should start to find usable compost at the bottom of the bin. To speed things up, stir and turn the compost with a trowel or fork every few weeks to add more air and help break down the materials. If you have added a lot of dry ingredients, water the compost occasionally to keep it moist.

When it's ready, compost material will be dark brown, broken down, earthy and nice smelling. Dig out what you need from the bottom of the bin, and chuck any remaining large lumps back in for some more time if needed. Use it all around the garden as a soil improver, mulch or to fill pots and trays for seedlings.

ORGANIC GARDENING 43

Organic practices have many benefits on the farm, including better soil, good yields with fewer chemicals, more wildlife and more jobs for farm workers. Many of these benefits can also be brought into your own garden. In particular, efforts to attract wildlife and support local birds will work all the better if you garden as organically as you can.

The six basic principles of organic gardening are:
1. Feed the soil, not the plants
2. Grow resistant and native varieties
3. Practise crop rotation, with different plants in different beds each year to preserve soil fertility
4. Do companion planting
5. Encourage predators, such as hedgehogs, to hunt down slugs
6. Use physical barriers, traps and netting to keep out pests

Be vigilant is another good principle. For pests and diseases prevention is better than cure and, often, simply removing and destroying leaves and branches where you first notice parasites taking up residence will keep them under control.

Companion planting puts species together that deter each other's pests or attract predators, such as dill and Californian poppies, with plants that suffer from aphids, as they attract hoverflies and ladybirds that eat aphids for breakfast!

44 MAKE FRIENDS WITH WILDLIFE

Your garden can be a real haven to help support sparrows, insects and other wildlife.

Feed the birds. Put out different seeds, fat cakes and nuts to attract a range of birds to your garden. Bird boxes and bird baths also provide essential help.

Plant bee-friendly flowers. Leave dandelions until they flower as an important early source of pollen, and look up which flowering plants are best to attract bees to your garden.

Support other insects. Buddleia is rightly known as the 'butterfly bush' and will grow easily in most gardens. Over winter, many insects need to hibernate. An 'insect hotel' can be made from a simple bunch of twigs in a plastic tube, left in a sheltered spot.

Plant a hedge. These are ideal for birds to nest and roost in, particularly sparrows, so create a new stretch of hedgerow by planting a number of different small trees and bushes together at the end of your garden.

Leave a wild corner. An out-of-the-way spot behind a hedge or next to the compost bin is ideal for leaving to go a bit wild. Add some rocks and dead wood to support toads, fungi and other creatures that like a bit of peace and darkness. You could also sow some native wildflowers or just see what grows.

45 USE WATER WISELY

Water used outside the home consumes seven per cent of the total tap water used by the average household, but at peak times in summer this can rise to more than 50 per cent.

Gorgeous, productive, relaxing gardens don't have to waste clean drinking water on a grand scale. More targeted watering, collecting rainwater and using grey water from the home can cut the amount your garden needs, and clever planting can also help.

Get a water butt for your garden. This collects rainwater from the gutters and stores it for dry days.

Use water wisely. Sprinklers and hoses can be really wasteful. Use a watering can or trigger hose and focus your efforts on the areas around your thirstiest plants rather than spraying a wide area. In a hot summer, let your lawn go brown (it will recover later).

Use 'grey water'. This is water that's been used for clean activities such as washing-up, baths and showers. This can be used to water the garden if you aren't using harsh cleaning chemicals.

Choose less thirsty plants. Put drought-resistant varieties in your borders. Shrubs with woody stalks put up with dry weather well, and other plants to try include catmint, rosemary, hardy geraniums, and peas and spinach in your vegetable patch.

ACTION

As you can tell from my CV, I've never been content to just try to change my own personal choices to help the environment, particularly when those choices are limited to terrible options because companies or governments aren't working to make greener options easier or cheaper.

You have more power than you think – both as a consumer and a citizen – so don't accept any limitations you find in what you can do to help the planet.

As an individual or working with others at work, at home or in your local community, you can persuade those with the power to decide to get on with making the changes you need. If something seems obvious to change, then make it happen and don't take no for an answer!

46 GREEN YOUR WORKPLACE

Workplaces can be a terrible drain on the world's resources. Super-busy business people don't always put the environment at the top of their concerns, and many opportunities to save energy aren't taken because people don't think it's part of their job.

If you're the boss, have influence, or can get a group of employees together to make a proposal, ask for a green plan for your workplace – just thinking about ways to save energy and resources means that good ideas from people on the ground have a chance of getting through. And being the one who comes up with the idea for a greener workplace plan could earn you respect for your long-term thinking, as well as a warm glow for making things a little bit better in the world.

Offices waste so much energy a year just from equipment left on outside office hours, so make sure your office has a policy of shutting things down before leaving. For office equipment, computers, printers and copiers, check the manual and find out how to make the lowest energy settings the default (get your resources department to send round a memo telling everyone how to do this). See about getting lighting put on motion sensors or timers and switched to low-energy LEDs. And don't forget to cut down on paper use and eliminate single-use plastics from activities like meetings, conferences and the office tea point.

A garage or workshop could be open to the elements and need heating to make work possible. Infrared directional lamps can provide heat in the right place only, saving lots of wasted energy.

47 BACK YOUR LOCAL HIGH STREET

High streets are vital to the health of our communities, providing essential goods within walking distance and places to meet and socialise. Small shops are also lower energy users than big stores that have open fridges, bright lights and harsh air conditioning. For each square metre of shopping space, a local grocer consumes up to three times less energy than a large supermarket.

Supporting local shops also helps the planet in other ways, by building a more resilient local economy where more of the money you spend stays in your area for longer.

I've put this topic in the 'action' chapter because your local high street may well need defending and supporting with more than just your custom.

Many high streets are suffering from too many empty shops and a poor street environment. While others are thriving, often thanks to a plan of action from the local community. Pop-ups in empty units, themed festivals and physical improvements, like wider pavements and reduced traffic, all make a real difference.

If your local shops need help, this is an ideal local campaign for residents to lead alongside shopkeepers. Your council and green groups can join in or give help and advice, and there are even some grants available here and there.

ACT WHEN YOU'RE OUT

48

Our leisure time accounts for a surprisingly high proportion of energy use – nearly a fifth. Activities like watching films and football matches, eating out or going to the gym don't directly involve burning fossil fuels. But related 'background' activities, especially food and drink at venues and the transport we use to get there, do add up to a lot.

For eating out, there are many more organic and green options now, but they still tend to be a bit exclusive. So, one way of taking really effective action is to encourage the places you already like to eat at to help the planet. This could be sourcing local food and drink, offering more meat-free options or doing away with bottled water. All of this makes a big difference and you often only have to ask to make a change happen.

And why not try activities that are closer to home and don't cost the earth? Go for a walk or bike ride instead of the gym, watch (or play in) your local sports teams or see local bands, comedy nights and theatre companies playing in pubs and small venues. And if these don't exist then why not really help by starting a team, club, band or creative venture yourself?

49 START A CAMPAIGN

There are so many examples of companies and governments making big changes thanks to campaigns started by people on the ground like you and me. If something's bugging you, if you've lost a bus service that was helping you get around, if your favourite company is being unnecessarily wasteful, or if a good idea simply isn't happening fast enough, take action and you can make a real difference.

Starting a campaign can be as easy as setting up a petition or writing a letter to a decision maker and asking your friends to do the same. Web tools, like facebook or twitter, and discussion websites like Mumsnet or Nextdoor, are great for gathering support. While a big change in policy can take years of pressure, some changes are so simple and easy that just a handful of letters can make them happen.

The fair trade movement is a great example of making a difference from the grassroots. This started out in the Netherlands in the 1980s and there are now shelves and shelves of fair trade products giving farmers a decent living from producing basic goods like coffee, tea, cocoa and sugar.

GET THE TOWN INVOLVED 50

Whole communities are getting together to make things better in all kinds of inspiring ways. And the more wide-ranging your plan and the more inspiring your vision, the easier it is to find ways to make changes together.

The village of Ashton Hayes in Cheshire is famous for setting a goal to become the first carbon-neutral village in England. Starting with a massive public meeting in 2006, they have already cut their carbon footprint more than 40 per cent, have ambitious plans for many aspects of their lives, and are funding for new carbon-neutral buildings. Residents have cut their personal travel, improved walking facilities, switched to local food supplies and are setting up their own energy company to take things even further.

Get inspiration and follow their progress at:
www.goingcarbonneutral.co.uk

The Transition Towns initiative also started out in 2006 in Totnes in Devon, and is now an international network of communities working on ways to be more self-sufficient and reduce their dependence on fossil fuels. Whole islands, towns and urban neighbourhoods in big cities are taking the initiative to make a difference and work more closely together.

Read more and find a whole load of useful resources at:
www.transitionnetwork.org

FURTHER INFORMATION & ADVICE

PLASTICS

RecycleNow has recycling information for the home, garden, workplaces, schools and other situations. It has interesting facts as well as some good tips.
www.recyclenow.com

The Waste & Resources Action Programme aims to improve how we use resources and reduce waste, and campaigns to reduce packaging as well as increase composting and recycling.
www.wrap.org.uk

Buy Me Once recommends long-lasting alternatives to throwaway products, including clothes, and has a good plastics section.
https://uk.buymeonce.com

The Natural Collection specialises in greener products and has loads of alternatives to plastic products, and some great gift ideas.
www.naturalcollection.com

Ecover detergents use the lowest impact ingredients, and you can get refills for their products at many green shops.
www.ecover.com

Lush shops are famous for reducing packaging and re-using their plastic pots.
www.lush.com

Green Fibres stocks organic and low-impact household essentials, including clothing, kitchen and bathroom accessories and even darning kits.
www.greenfibres.com

People Tree – the original fair-trade clothing label
www.peopletree.co.uk

Who made my clothes? This Fashion Revolution campaign works for higher ethical standards in the fashion industry.
www.fashionrevolution.org

Oxfam lets you buy charity gifts via their 'unwrapped' website
www.oxfam.org/en/oxfam-unwrapped

The Kimberly Process certifies conflict-free diamonds.
www.kimberleyprocess.com

Some places to find eco-friendly baby clothes and products:
www.spiritofnature.co.uk
www.earthlets.co.uk

ENERGY

The Energy Saving Trust has advice on energy saving and links to available sources of grants to help with insulation.
www.energysavingtrust.org.uk

The HEAT project website provides a clear and simple guide to grants and support for home energy-saving and insulation.
www.heatproject.co.uk

The National Energy Foundation has advice on saving electricity.
www.nef.org.uk

The Centre for Alternative Technology in Wales has a wealth of advice on energy saving and green electricity.
www.cat.org.uk

The Waterwise website is a fantastic online resource for water-saving tips.
www.waterwise.org.uk

Power Up North London is my local community energy project, and shows what you can achieve with a great group of people behind your efforts.
www.powerupnorthlondon.org

Ethical Consumer has guides to the greenest products across a very wide range of industries, including an assessment of green energy tariffs.
www.ethicalconsumer.org

These campaigners are working on divestment and can tell you which companies and funds to avoid putting your pension into.
www.350.org
www.gofossilfree.org

Freecycle – find a local group offering free things in your area, or find a good home for your unwanted items.
www.freecycle.org

The Australian Government has an excellent energy savings advice website.
www.yourenergysavings.gov.au

TRAVEL

Living Streets has been promoting walking for 85 years. They have a massive amount of information for helping make walking easier and safer.
www.livingstreets.org.uk

The Ramblers aren't just about country walks. They have guides to city walking, campaign for safe routes and access, and have a wealth of information and advice for walkers at all levels.
www.ramblers.org.uk

Cycling UK is the UK's largest national cycling organisation, founded in 1878 and still helping cyclists and promoting better cycle routes today.
www.cyclinguk.org

Traveline is where you can look up local bus timetables anywhere in the UK.
www.traveline.info

Bikeability is the cycling award scheme for children in the UK, with online advice and activities for kids and parents.
www.bikeability.org.uk

Greener Journeys is a campaign to get more people using the bus or coach for their trips.
www.greenerjourneys.com

In London, don't simply hop on the Tube. Find out your other options, including trams, riverboats and thousands of buses, using Transport for London's journey planner or the Citymapper app. Both services can find you good routes by foot or bike as well.
www.tfl.gov.uk
www.citymapper.com

Carplus and Bikeplus is a charity promoting responsible car use and shared transport, with a map of car clubs and shared bike services across the UK.
www.carplusbikeplus.org.uk

Information about greener cars and alternative fuel vehicles available in the UK is brought together at Next Green Car.
www.nextgreencar.com

Find people to share your journeys on the Liftshare website.
www.liftshare.org

The Energy Saving Trust gives advice to organisations and businesses on workplace travel plans and greener business travel.
http://www.energysavingtrust.org.uk/transport-travel

The website for Scotland's national tourist board has lots of information on things to see and do in Scotland.
www.visitscotland.com

Wales has some amazing unspoilt sites. Find out more at its tourism website.
www.visitwales.com

Northern Ireland can be reached easily by ferry and has some spectacular coastline and sights. They even have a special guide to the many Game of Thrones filming locations in the country!
www.discovernorthernireland.com

And not to forget England, which has plenty to see too.
www.visitengland.com

The Man in Seat 61 website has a wealth of practical advice for booking non-flying travel tickets all over the world, including trains across Europe.
www.seat61.com

In response to concerns about offsetting, WWF and other green organisations set up the Gold Standard, which aims to make sure only real, useful, projects are certified for credit in offsetting emissions. Read more about the issues on the project's website
www.goldstandard.org

COOKING & EATING

Sustain is an organisation that promotes fairer and greener farming, and which produces 'food facts' reports about a range of environmental issues.
www.sustainweb.org

The Soil Association has loads of information on greener and organic consumption and things you can do to help.
www.soilassociation.org

Love Food Hate Waste has plenty of recipes for leftovers
www.lovefoodhatewaste.com

The Vegetarian Society provides tips to help you eat less meat, as well as a host of good recipes.
www.vegsoc.org

The Vegan Society has a wide range of advice on avoiding all animal products, and their recipes are delicious.
www.vegansociety.com

The BBC Food's recipe archive has many excellent vegetarian and vegan recipes.
www.bbc.com/food

The Women's Institute is always campaigning and giving advice on how to be greener, and has a big campaign on food waste.
www.thewi.org.uk

FARMA represents local farmers across the UK and helps you find your nearest farm shops and farmers' markets.
www.farma.org.uk

IN THE GARDEN

Garden Organic – from the Henry Doubleday Research Association.
www.gardenorganic.org.uk

The Soil Association has lots of info on better gardening as well as better food.
www.soilassociation.org

BBC Gardening online
www.bbc.co.uk/gardening

The RSPB has a wildlife gardening guide that will help bring birds back into your garden.
www.rspb.org.uk

Wild About Gardens from The Wildlife Trusts has the answer to almost every question about local wildlife and your garden.
www.wildaboutgardens.org

Buglife focuses on gardening to help insects – a really important part of our ecosystem.
www.buglife.org.uk

ACTION

Friends of the Earth work internationally but also have local groups taking action in your area.
www.foe.org

Greenpeace work incredibly hard to bring issues to our attention and get real green action. They have local groups who can help with your issues as well.
www.greenpeace.org.uk

I used to work at Campaign for Better Transport and they have lots of resources to help you start a local campaign for improved public transport.
www.bettertransport.org.uk

The Carbon Trust has tools to help workplaces put together plans and measure the impact of energy savings.
www.carbontrust.com

NEON provides an incredible range of training and organising tools to help you be more effective in your campaigns.
www.neweconomyorganisers.org

Mumsnet is a massive online community for women in the UK.
www.mumsnet.com

Nextdoor brings local communities together to discuss issues and solve problems in your neighbourhood.
www.nextdoor.co.uk

The FairTrade Foundation has resources and guides for how to convert more organisations to buying fairly traded goods
www.fairtrade.org.uk